# RELEASE
# Your Kid's Dormant
# GENIUS
# in Just 10 Minutes a Day

## PARENTING YOUR SMART UNDERACHIEVER WITH CONSISTENCY AND LOVE

### BY MICHAL STAWICKI

www.expandbeyondyourself.com

2

September 2014
Copyright © 2014 Michal Stawicki
All rights reserved worldwide.
ISBN: 150868037X
ISBN-13: 978- 1508680376

# Table of Contents

# Disclaimer

I'm not an American. In an attempt to make the book more readable for you, I've "Americanized" the most 'native' parts of this book. I've changed some subjects' names. In Poland, we have a different scale of school grades; I translated it into what's most common in the USA.

My elder son's name is Krzysztof and it's pronounced as "Cshishtoff," but in English, it's Christopher. My younger son's name is written in Polish differently than in English - Nataniel.

This is the 3rd book in the series and there is some redundancy in the second chapter, between this one and both *Learn to Read with Great Speed* and *The Fitness Expert Next Door*, so if you read them – be aware.

1

# Introduction

If you don't know yet, you will discover in Chapter Two that I'm a firm believer in the results of any sustained action. But this belief alone wouldn't be enough to make me share the intimacy of my family life. There was an event which I cannot erase from my memory, and I just need to share my experience, if I want to keep the peace of my soul.

During the past school year, my younger son, Nathaniel, at the age of 10, had some problems with his school education: mediocre grades, neglected homework, unprepared for lessons many times. The situation was new to me – my elder son has never had any troubles learning. I decided to pay more attention to Nathaniel's education. I noticed his problems with proper spelling, reading and writing, and decided to pay a visit to the professionals at the Learning Disabilities Service Center.

The first step was our joint interview with an educationist. I remember me explaining my son's difficulties and the measures I took to help him overcome them. Simple things: doing homework together, giving reading assignments, learning words in a foreign language. And then the pedagogue[1] said something which disturbed me very much:

"It's not common to see such a commitment from a parent."

At first, I felt admirable: what a good parent I am, ho, ho, ho! But in the same second, I realized I was doing nothing spectacular, just something every parent would do in my place, wouldn't they? I was perplexed. The educationist lady has been dealing with troubled children and their parents for years, that's her job. Did she really mean what she said? I looked her in the eyes. She was serious.

A shocking realization struck me: it is something exceptional to take care of your child. To support him, to help him, to be with him.

There are plenty of excuses for such a situation and I went through most of them: I don't have time; that's the teachers' job, they are paid for it; I have other responsibilities and family members to take care of; he is just a kid, it's just a primary school, he will deal with it when he grows up; I'm exhausted.

I used them until the circumstances got dramatic and I had to face the truth. Those excuses were meant

---

[1] Educationist, teacher.

to comfort me in my laziness, not to improve my son's situation.

And I found the truth. Regarding Nathaniel's education, I should be the most interested man in the universe. There is no one else who can replace me in that position. Who should be more interested? Maybe his teachers, a school pedagogue, a school psychologist? For them, he could be just a part of their job. And they can live with such an attitude. They have their problems, families and priorities, too. They may be more qualified, but as a father, I should be the man who cares most about my son's future.

And he is too young to understand the consequences of neglecting his education. I know what I'm talking about, I didn't start to be serious about **my** education until my university studies.

The interview with the educationist steeled my determination. No matter how busy I am, how tired, if I don't care about his progress, nobody else will. I decided to keep my commitment for as long as it takes. Before the interview, I was set more for a quick fix than a regular program. I thought I would get him out of the woods and go back to my activities.

And I strongly suppose that's the attitude of the majority of parents, and the reason for the pedagogue's remark.

I stuck to the simple things we were doing together with Nathaniel to help him. And the outcome was simply amazing. There was a moment when he more than doubled his reading speed (I let him off the hook; he walked out on reading training and his results worsened almost immediately). His command of English improved drastically; he even took part in a school English contest. But what is most important, he finished the school year with honors. I really didn't expect that.

It didn't take me much time daily to teach him, help him with homework, examine him. I just couldn't find more time - I work and commute almost 12 hours every working day. My son is important to me, but he is not the center of my world. His education is not the most important factor in raising him, there is also spirituality and health - more significant considerations for me. Besides, I have two more kids, a wife, bills to pay and so on, and so on. I can't recall supervising his education taking me more than one hour any given day – sometimes, it has been literally just a couple of minutes.

And it worked, the results came. Why? Check out the second chapter.

2

# Ten Minutes

**I** **KNOW that daily, sustained action brings results.**

I know it because I practice this rule in many areas of my life. I focus daily on specific actions, committing 10 minutes to them. I track my results. And I see them improving. I've gotten results in such different areas as weight loss, finances, learning skills and relationships. I strongly suppose that it is a universal law applicable to absolutely ALL areas of life.

If you do something daily and you are not getting the desired results, it simply means you are putting at least as much daily and sustained effort against those results. The more action, the better results, up to some reasonable level - take a look at a chart below.

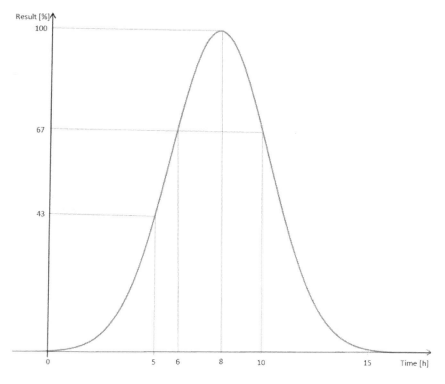

The shape of the curve is called normal distribution in probability research. It is, in statistics, something like a number π in math. As π can be found in many equations describing the texture of the universe, normal distribution can be used to describe a multitude of quantities in physics and measurements in biology, including IQ, height, weight and many more. According to the central limit theorem, the mean of a large number of random variables tends to normal distribution. And in our big and complicated world, a lot of effects are presented by a large number of random data. I did study the statistics (years ago) and still don't understand most of this stuff, and it's out of the scope of this book, anyway. If you are curious, it is

explained in a forthright way here:
http://askville.amazon.com/Central-Limit-THeorem-apply-statistics-life/AnswerViewer.do?requestId=7620607

I believe the normal distribution can be also applied to describe a relation between a human effort represented by time and achieved results. We have to sleep, so we have about 16 hours at our disposal, and we can get the maximum result by investing half of them in one activity. If we give less time, we don't achieve the maximum result, and if we dedicate too much time, we are burning out. In the case of teaching a kid, it is quite possible that the optimum time is much shorter than 8 hours - a child just cannot stay focused for that long.

But you are not going to devote 8 hours a day of your precious life to get a maximum result, which in this case would be ... a top of the class student in the state, I suppose. All you need is just to pay some more attention to your kid's education. Check out the zoomed left part of the chart.

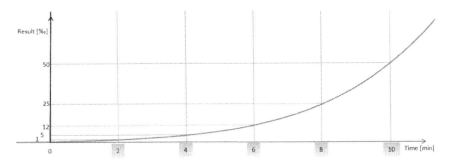

Even the smallest amount of invested time brings results. I use consciously about two minutes of my day on savings and I do a few monthly activities - a budget summary, paying bills, dividing my resources between different assets and so on. It takes me about 2 hours so, overall, it's six minutes a day. And it brings me the results. I save almost five times more than a year ago.

Ten minutes is just a handy number. It can be two minutes and you still will get the results. They will be just microscopic scale results and their compounded effect will take 50 times longer than if you use 10 minutes.

Every - even the tiniest - sustained action brings results.

That's the core philosophy and it overcomes two major obstacles of any lasting change: fear of failure, which stops us even before we begin, and giving up, which stops us after we begin, but before we get satisfying results.

**Every** action brings results in the end. As long as you do something, you can't fail. There is no failure. You have nothing to fear. You can begin without the burden of hesitations and doubts.

And giving up is out of the question. What can make you want to resign, if you **know** that the results are guaranteed, that all you need to do is just to sustain your action? Giving up is not like early withdrawal, where you get your money back and sometimes even a part of interest. It's like being in an investment program. Your obligation is to invest $1,000 every month and if you do it for 5 years, you will get your $60,000 of capital and guaranteed $40,000 of the return on investment. However, if you break the agreement you will get only part of your capital - from 10% in the first year of a contract, to 50% in the last year - and none of the returns.

I'm fond of this simile, as it's not only about the process of getting results, but also what you are going to do when you achieve them. After 5 years, you can decide on what to do with your money. You can put all of it back into the investment program again or you can just spend everything. It's the same with supervising your kid's education. You can make homework and additional assignments, and fix his/her grades. Then, you stop for a few months and guess what happens? He or she is in trouble again. Or you can continue to work together and instill the proper learning habits in your child.

"All right" - you may say - "but those are some fancy stories and theories. How is it applicable in my life?" I concur, theorization is quite useless. What caused me to embrace this philosophy wasn't other's stories and preaching. It was my stories.

In order to feel at a gut level that it is indeed a universal law, applicable also to you, please give a thought to any successful area of your life. It can be anything - your marriage, a specific skill, a career, the fact that you have never had a car accident, good grades at school, patience, your great relationship with your parents ... the best thing for this little exercise will be something you take for granted, but other people are praising you for. So, pick one and think: what makes you successful in this area? What's the difference between you and the people who praise you, who aren't successful? What do you do that they don't?

I bet you will find some sustained action underlying your success.

I take the love in my family for granted. I hadn't noticed it until my newfound online friends drew my attention to it, by their comments on my personal blog. I have given it some thought and discovered that I say "I love you" to my wife and kids every day. When I was a teenager, I realized that in my family those words were ... well, maybe not a taboo, but close to it. I didn't hear those words very often in my home. And I was missing it. So I decided in my heart, that when I start **my** family, I will say this to **my** family members as often as I feel like it. It happened to be every day. In fact, several times each day. And this simple action makes all the difference in our family life.

And it's just one instance of this law. I found many other examples behind my big and small successes - the high school diploma, the scholarship on the 4th year of university studies, my personal fitness records.

It is true. You will find such examples in your life, too.

Look at the time/results chart once again. You probably noticed how the results grow exponentially after some point. As I said earlier - the more time you invest, the better results you get. I'm just assuming that your time and energy level is limited. You have the whole family to take care of, bills to pay, work to do, people to help, projects to attend to, relationships to keep or improve. You have more pressing matters to take care of. You have only 24 hours and it's hard to find time for anything else. Thus, 10 minutes.

# 3

---

# Recognizing the Problems

When you are trying to help out with your kid's learning for the first time, you need to recognize and work on his/her weak spots. At least, my experience confirms that this approach bears good fruits. I focused on improving Nathaniel's weak spots. This method not only enhanced those particular skills and areas he had troubles with, but it also brought the overall improvement of his school situation.

Did you ever fail and were disappointed by your results? Did you ever put yourself in a self-criticism spiral? Well, kids have the same inner critic's mechanisms, and it works in the case of their school results, too: "I suck at English. I'll never learn it. I'm a failure. I don't want to learn it anymore; it's pointless." So when we improved the areas he didn't feel confident in, his horizon expanded. I observed his childish joy when he understood English enough to construct simple sentences, or when he doubled his reading speed.

His inner talk changed, too. He discovered he can learn, he can improve, he can achieve more, even in areas where he didn't think he could. Because of this new attitude, he corrected grades in not only a few subjects, but virtually all the subjects.

Do not try to improve your child's strong points to instill more confidence in him/her or whatever the reason you've come up with. I think it's fine and good, a noble intent, but only if you have time and resources for such activities. As I said in the previous chapter, I assume you have enough on your plate and it's hard for you to find more time to take care of your kid's teaching. And I assure you, your child will cope with his strong points, breaking no sweat.

My son is very good in math. He was 26th in the countrywide competition (I don't know the exact number, but there were several tens of thousands of competitors). Regarding math, he knows his value and has been getting "As" for most of his life. His small successes fueled his confidence. His motivation was (and still is) high. He didn't need my help in that area.

However, I could train him to be even better. I saw that with some consistency, he could achieve more, but then I wouldn't have any time for training his other skills, the ones which desperately cried for improvement.

I don't know about you, how much you know about your kid's struggles, but I didn't really know what the exact problems were regarding my son's education. I had some vague concepts and they weren't even far from the reality - for example, I knew he despised reading, but I had no idea how poorly he read. What I mean is that I was familiar with his problem areas - calligraphy, reading, spelling, fluent speech, English (a foreign language for him). I just didn't realize the full scope of his problems.

And the same may be true in your case. You know what's wrong - sometimes it's enough to take a look at a child's grades to know that - but you don't know the details. So get to know them.

You don't need fancy tests or professional counseling. Not that they don't work or would be harmful - it's just an additional fuss, time and resources to sacrifice, and you can use this time to start immediately. I needed more than a month to reserve an appointment at the Learning Disabilities Service. It would be wasted time if I just sat on my hands that whole period.

I started doing Nathaniel's homework with him regularly. I think it's the easiest and most efficient way to get familiar with your child's level of skills and knowledge. He/she must do it anyway, so why not use this as an excuse to get some useful intel? And my experience is that the kid's problems are not enormous. Every adult would recognize and deal with them with ease. Let's take a look at what I found out about my son's weak spots:

- Reading - I had just started my speed reading training then, so I checked Nathaniel's reading speed out of curiosity. He read only 71 words per minute! I found the source of all his troubles with reading by this single masterstroke. The slower you read, the less you comprehend (at least it's true up to about 200 words per minute). He read so slowly that he couldn't follow the references for math exercises. He generally didn't read any exercise's description; he had been guessing or asking schoolmates and teachers for the meaning.

— English - I knew he was not very good at it, but he had been getting "B" most of the times, sometimes "Cs" and occasionally even an "A". Frankly, I don't know how he got them. Was it his cleverness? Or the fact that he had about five different English teachers during the first three years? I discovered that he knew just a handful of words, maybe five dozen. He had no idea how to construct a negative sentence – he didn't even know how to alter "to be."

— Spelling - Polish is a difficult language with native characters and complicated writing rules. Nathaniel had problems with them, too, but he had even been writing people's and place's names with small letters. It's not that he didn't know the rules, he just completely ignored them.

— Calligraphy - it is enough to say that many times he couldn't decipher his own writing.

— Fluent speech - I found his vocabulary was very poor. Mostly because he didn't read. It also caused him problems with other subjects, like history or biology. He tended to use colloquial language all too often and he oversimplified his statements.

As you can see, it isn't rocket science. Those are a primary school student's problems. They are relatively easy to face. But first, I needed to recognize them and their scale. I was able to locate them by simply doing the homework with him for a couple of weeks.

Do the same. Find a bottom line, the source of your child's difficulties. It may be trouble with focus, with counting, with reading, lack of basic skills or knowledge. Whatever the reason is, find it. Only then can you help him/her effectively.

# 4

---

# Tactics

The particular tactics I used to overcome my son's problems may not be the ones you need to apply in the case of your child. I just want you to take a look at my approach and come up with your own tactics. Of course, if your kid has the exact difficulties as mine (for example, slow reading), those tactics are directly applicable for you, too.

## First and foremost - homework

I've already mentioned the first advantage of doing homework together in the previous chapter - recognizing the problem areas. But there are a lot more advantages than just that.

Nathaniel is smart, but lazy. Only a small part of his troubles came from lack of knowledge or skill. Most of the times, he just didn't do his homework, because he had more interesting things to do (read: playing with his mates).

He was 10 years old; he wasn't a baby to watch his every step. So we worked out the new procedure for doing homework: he did it after school, and when I came back from work, I marked it. Sometimes he would leave some difficult exercise undone, counting on my help (I almost cured him of this habit after several months of doing homework together). Then we worked on the problem areas, the things he couldn't understand. Later on, he was correcting the homework according to my suggestions. Lastly, I made the final revision.

That procedure puts the most work on his shoulders. All in all, it was his homework and his responsibility. On the other hand, I could focus on what's important - teaching when he couldn't grasp some concepts and on correcting mistakes. There were days when it took us up to one hour, but there were days when we dealt with the homework within five minutes.

Doing homework together was also an excellent occasion to work on his writing (spelling and calligraphy), unobtrusively. It happened just by the way. Many times, I couldn't read what he wrote, and in such cases he was supposed to write the unreadable word in his calligraphy exercise book. And I was checking his spelling in the process.

I observed his carelessness in the way he did his lessons. He just wanted to get rid of the duty and go to the more fun activities. The quality of his work always suffered because of this attitude. The writing exercises were a great way to train his temper. Gradually, he learned to do his homework slowly and carefully, focusing on the job, so he didn't have to repeat the process again and again correcting his writing and mistakes.

I want you to get the full importance of such a basic activity as doing homework together. Take a look of the list of advantages once again:

- gathering information about your kid's skills, knowledge, weak spots and mannerisms
- an occasion to work on basic skills, like spelling and calligraphy
- a way to learn self-discipline and consistency (for both of you)
- nipping the child's mistakes and misbehaviors in the bud and on the fly
- a chance to spend time together and strengthen your relationship (and we all know that rules without relationship is a recipe for rebellion, don't we?)

## Reading

I'm a firm believer of consistent and continuous practice. I also found that many of my son's difficulties come from his poor reading capability. He neglected this skill, he just did what was necessary to survive in a school environment and nothing more. I dread to think at what level are the reading skills of other kids from his class, the ones who got mostly "Cs", not "Bs".

Anyway, Nathaniel's vocabulary was poor. His spelling, storytelling and speaking abilities suffered because of that. His pronouncements were extremely clumsy for such a smart 10-year-old boy.

The remedy was simple - a daily reading assignment. At the beginning, he had to read just several pages a day, usually about five. As I mentioned in the second chapter, he read very slowly. Three years after learning reading, he still murmured while reading. In egghead's language, it's called sub-vocalization, and had a devastating impact on his reading speed.

Sub-vocalization, or silent speech, is defined as the internal speech made when reading a word, thus allowing the reader to imagine the sound of the word as it is read. This is a natural process when reading. Sub-vocalization is popularly associated with moving one's lips, the actual term refers primarily to the movement of muscles associated with speaking, not the literal moving of lips. Well, his silent speech wasn't so silent after all; he really moved his lips while reading.

So I introduced some basic speed reading techniques into his reading training. There are some advanced and difficult methods, but I made him use the simplest one first - biting his tongue and pursing his lips.

I gradually increased the scope of his assignments, but not very much. Every day, Nathaniel reads a chapter of a book, four to 12 pages. What is important, and what makes this simple task bring such great results, is consistency. He has read every single day since October 2012. Or almost every day - he tried to cheat by telling me he read that day, when he really didn't.

I understand him. He hated reading and he still doesn't enjoy it very much. It's normal; I also don't like to do things I'm not good at. But in modern society, an aversion to reading is as ridiculous as an aversion to breathing. So we needed to get past his moods. After several cases of "amnesia" regarding his reading assignment, I started to demand a report from the story. And you know what? That gave me an ideal chance to improve his storytelling. I listen to the stories told by him and I correct him on the fly. I show him how better wording could be used in this or that particular sentence. I make him wonder about the word's meaning.

In my other book, "Learn to Read with Great Speed," I told the whole fascinating story of Nathaniel's reading adventure. Let me just state that there was a moment when he almost tripled his reading speed. He has also read all seven parts of "The Chronicles of Narnia," and four other books during the training process. This is more than 70% of what adult Americans have read in 2012[2]. And it's just 10 months, in his case.

I give much credit for his overall improvement to this mundane task. He reads faster now, he understands more of what he reads and his vocabulary has expanded. It all had an impact on his other subjects, not just Polish. He can follow the references in math exercises now ;)

---

[2] http://libraries.pewinternet.org/2012/12/27/e-book-reading-jumps-print-book-reading-declines/

# English

We started learning English almost from scratch. Nathaniel had taken the line of least resistance in his English classes. He is just a genius at avoiding the work. So he found a way to hardly know English at all and still get good (well, not very bad) grades. My son learned the basics of basics. He knew the differences in phonetic spelling between English and Polish and a handful of words.

I'm no educationist. I don't know efficient techniques for teaching a foreign language. And I had no time to learn them. But I knew that consistently applied effort brings results. So the sole method I used was teaching him new English words. Of course, there were occasions to teach some grammar and rules while doing homework, but the foreign language program, as such, came down to mostly teaching new words.

At the beginning, I made him write out about 30 words and he was learning them each day. When he tackled that material, I obligated him to write down and learn three new words a day. And I examined him almost every day. We took breaks from adding new words when I observed that it was too much for him to absorb. In such cases, he stopped adding new words for a few days and focused on learning those he had already written down before. I also made him memorize alternations of "to be" and "to have."

In order not to overwhelm him, we took breaks for holidays, too. During the summer holidays, he has to learn just one new word each day.

And that's it. He is still far away from being familiar with English, nothing to say about fluency, but he has many more skills regarding foreign language than he had before. He knows the difference between singular and plural, between first and third person. He can construct sentences, including negative and interrogative ones.

He took part in a school contest, without any success worth mentioning, but the participation alone was a success. It was an indicator that his teacher saw the improvement.

# 5

---

# Tips

## Consistency is the key

I mean, you need to be consistent and demand from yourself. Never give up. You may have the impression that all my methods were implemented smoothly and without many difficulties. Well, they weren't.

Beware of the "everything is gonna be all right" feeling. It's not going to be all right, unless you make it all right. Consistency is a key factor that brings the results. I neglected my discipline of checking Nathaniel's progress about a dozen times, based on a false hope that he grasped it already, that he would continue on his own from now on. He didn't and he won't. It was my laziness and neediness of comfort which inspired those breaks, not the real effects of our work.

Every time I neglected this discipline, I observed my son slacking off almost immediately. When he knew I was going to ask him about the story he read, examine him on English words and so on, he had to be constantly prepared. But when he noticed I wasn't paying attention, he was more than happy to take care of his "business" - watching cartoons, playing with mates, playing the computer - instead of learning. He again took the line of least resistance.

If you are tired, exhausted and say to yourself, "I'll skip it, just this one time," remember that your child is more than eager to skip it one, two times and keep skipping it forever. That's why you started in the first place. It's your responsibility to keep going; the kid's cooperation is reluctant, at best.

It's not really **what** you are doing with your kid that matters, it's the consistency. My experience shows that you don't have to do **everything,** every time. The bottom line is to do something every day. So, when I was exhausted, I only examined Nathaniel's English vocabulary. Or I asked him about the story read today. Or I checked his homework.

Just remember to switch every so often between activities. Kids are amazingly adaptable and tend towards the line of least resistance. Nathaniel does not even do it purposefully. As I said before, during the summer holidays, he was obligated to read a chapter of a book and learn a single English word a day. But when he noticed I didn't check on his English words for a few days, or I didn't ask him to tell me today's story from a book, it immediately wasn't his priority. He postponed it for later in the day, and if I didn't remind him - he didn't do it that day at all.

## Put the majority of the work on your child's shoulders

My ultimate goal was to make my son's learning process more independent, so I wouldn't have to supervise him around the clock. And I think that's the goal of every sensible parent. We cannot be there for them to help and teach them for the rest of their lives. The purpose of all this fuss is to make them self-sufficient, isn't it? So I structured the learning program in a way that made him do most of the work. For example, during summer vacation he read for about 15 minutes, he studied English for several minutes and I examined him for a few minutes. He does 80% of the job alone and 20% with my help.

Remember - you are the one with the job to go to, bills to pay and all the other adult responsibilities. The majority of your work is simply to supervise. It's your son/daughter who has to do the major chunk of the job. Don't do his/her homework, don't read his/her books, don't bother yourself with details such as which exact new words should he/she learn now. Your child is perfectly capable of doing all those things.

Your goal is to improve the knowledge and skills of your kid. It's not going to happen if he/she doesn't stretch, doesn't grow. That's another reason to put most of the work on his/her shoulders. Of course, beware of overdoing, of putting too much on him/her – they are just kids, after all.

In addition, if you are as busy as I assume, you won't have time to supervise every assignment you put on him/her, if you give too many of them. That's another advantage of the 10-minute philosophy, in the case of teaching children. It's just as much as you can do in such a short time span, so it's not likely you'll demand too much.

## Making the learning process interesting

I don't know about you, but when I was a kid, I wasn't motivated by the perspective of good grades. Yeah, it was nice to get them, but it wasn't the prospect of getting an "A" which kept me in front of the books.

Anyone would go crazy after some time, if he had to work day after day on tasks he hates. Kids need diversity and something more than duty to keep their focus. That's why Nathaniel had to read not only the school lectures, but also The Chronicles of Narnia, which he found interesting. I did also give him some reading assignments from the Encyclopedia of Animals, because he loves all kinds of creatures. He hates reading anyway, but this task was a little more bearable for him when having something more engaging to read.

Don't make your child memorize everything the way it is taught in textbooks. I found language, even in the primary school textbooks, overly orotund, dry and cerebral. Try to explain the things your kid doesn't understand in simpler terms or using life examples. I want for my son to understand the material in a way he is capable of absorbing, not just to get better grades at school. And it's more effective, anyway. He just doesn't grasp any academic terms.

For example: hillock in his Natural Science textbook is defined as: "a terrain elevation having up to 50 meters of the relative altitude." And I said: "It's a small hill, sonny."

Try to introduce an element of play or challenge into the learning process. Your child is out of kindergarten, so there doesn't need to be a lot of play, but a pinch here and there can only help. Learning just for the sake of learning has a hypnotizing, numbing effect on the mind. I'm not good at playing while teaching, but I made a joke from time to time when discussing the story read today by my son. Or I used a funny example to illustrate my point, while explaining some natural science phenomena. Well, the best fun we had was when we tried to decipher his writing. We invented a lot of funny words then.

As to the challenges, I made it a contest between my sons a few times. They were examining each other's knowledge of English words. Including my older son made a family activity out of an otherwise mundane job. It also stirred up some excitement in Nathaniel. And the best of it? I was freed from examining him myself and I could do something else.

Even if you have only one child you can introduce the element of challenge. Your kid just needs to be challenged against himself/herself. Which brings me to the next tip: set goals, rewards and punishments. It worked perfectly in the case of reading practice with my son. I set a specific word-per-minute goal for him to achieve by the end of each month of practice. If he succeeded, he did reap a reward we both agreed upon -

more time to play outside, more time to play on the computer and so forth. If he failed, he got something less pleasurable, like additional household duties. Again, we discussed the punishment in advance and we both agreed on it.

I set goals which made him stretch, struggle. On the 18th of October, he read 71 words per minute. By the end of the month, I wanted him to read 100 wpm. He did it and he got ungrounded. Then I set him a 130 wpm limit for the end of November. He succeeded again and was allowed more time to play on the computer and, most importantly, he was happy about himself, because he achieved something extraordinary - at least for him. We made a different arrangement for December, as it was the month of winter holidays: he just had to keep his reading speed of 130 wpm. We agreed on no reward, but he would get a punishment if he slacked off.

Just keep in mind that you must be prepared for both eventual reward and punishment. Don't agree on five additional hours on the computer or your kid won't have time for doing homework. And if you plan some sanction, make sure you are willing and able to enforce it.

I made an agreement with Nathaniel for a particular month, that if he didn't reach the specific words-per-minute limit, he would have to play with his younger sister every day for the next month. He failed to accomplish it and I had an additional duty - keeping watch on his new obligation.

## Follow the kid's new lessons

Don't restrict yourself to his/her current homework. It's also helpful to ask your child what new information he/she has learned today and check if he/she understood the new material. In Poland, this task is easier for a parent, as kids carry their textbooks in their backpack all the time. I just needed to go through Nathaniel's backpack every day, take all his textbooks out and have him show me his last lesson. Then I skipped through it, asked him a few questions and immediately I knew which part he grasped and which he didn't. And it was an additional opportunity to correct his speaking manners and vocabulary.

Your child can have a backlog of knowledge to catch up on, but it is important that he/she can keep up the pace with ongoing material, too. It will make your life easier in the long run. You won't have to play catch-up forever, but just to the point at which you started.

## It's hard to start, but it's easy to keep the momentum going

The setup of our teaching sessions was a nightmare. For the first couple of weeks, it took me about an hour a day to go through various activities - check new lessons, mark the homework, examining English words and more. I needed to tame a "wild beast" - my son was not used to regular practice sessions. At all.

Be very careful in this initial period. Do not deplete your motivation too fast. Keep in mind that it's just temporary. Once you implement the teaching process and make a habit of it both for your kid and for you, it will get easier. As Johann Wolfgang von Goethe said: "Everything is hard before it's easy".

You can read more about willpower and motivation depletion on a very interesting blog about habit development: DevelopGoodHabits.

Anyway, it **really** gets easier after some time. You and your child will be more proficient in your tasks. Then, you start to win over his/her problems one by one. The backlog will decrease. Step by step, you will move forward and time commitment will decrease, too.

After the initial period of intense work, I restricted some activities, like going through Nathaniel's backpack (and new lessons) to about once, twice a week. After a couple of months of calligraphy exercises, he became more careful and he wrote a little better. I became more accustomed to his writing style. I could finally read what he wrote ;) And we stopped those exercises altogether.

He didn't get homework every day, so we were free from this activity every second, third day. Gradually, more often than not, the teaching tasks took me 10 minutes or less.

Then we could schedule some bigger chunks of the teaching program for weekends, when I had more time for him.

It all looked overwhelming only at the beginning. All in all, those were just a primary school student's problems. They are easy to deal with by an adult!

## Be a good example

It's almost the last tip, but not least. Integrity is not something you can lecture into your child. You have to show it. You don't just show him/her that you care, you **must** care, to be able to show it.

I repeat to my son, time after time, the sentence: "Your duties go first; your pleasures go second." That's the rule I want to instill in him for the rest of his life. And as soon as I don't practice what I preach, he goes for his pleasures first. Especially if the duty in question is our teaching program. Every time I neglected my commitment in the process, his commitment dropped rapidly, too.

I don't know if you are familiar with "The 7 Habits of Highly Effective People" book. Its author, Stephen R. Covey, explains the concept of Circle of Influence as "the things you can do something about" against the concept of the Circle of Concern - things you are worried about, but have no real control over, like global warming or the national debt.

It's easy to mistake those circles in the case of teaching your child. Trust me, I know something about it. You probably assume - like almost everybody - that the homework of your kid is in your circle of influence.

Wrong!

You can't do his/her homework. It's your child's job. You can force your kid to do the homework once, twice, several times, but the expenditure of power is so much greater than the results you get. So, you must seek to find things you can do something about. Your job is to focus on them. I found that out the hard way and I share it, so you won't repeat my mistakes.

I discovered that Nathaniel's homework concerns me, but I can't actually do it for him or with him. I found I can do other things - check on him every day, remind him about the homework, mark it if done. That was (and still is) my responsibility.

Don't repeat my mistakes. Keep in mind that you are an adult, a leader in this partnership and it's your responsibility to keep the momentum going. The best way to deal with it, is to make a habit out of it - an automatic activity you don't have to ponder much upon. And remember: focus on the things **you** can do something about.

## Trigger & tracking

Schedule a block of time for each day. I would suggest at least an hour for the initial week. If it takes less time - fine. Rephrasing the old saying - it's better to reserve too much time and not need it than to reserve too little and not have enough.

A very useful tool for habit creation is a trigger. If you have any common ritual already established with your child - cleaning the room after school, watching a favorite cartoon together - use it as an introduction to a teaching session. If your daily schedule is moderately routine, it's easier. The ideal solution is to schedule this block of time at the same hour every day.

However, the world we live in is not ideal. My schedule is hectic. I work different shifts, sometimes overtime at night, and I need to sleep during the day, so regular hours for my work with Nathaniel are out of the question. What helped me to keep a consistency was a tracking system, the most basic of all imaginable - pen and paper.

I already track some of my daily activities this way. I prepare a piece of paper, write the names of activities in the first column, the days of the week or month in the columns' header and check them off when I fulfill a specific obligation. I just added "Nathaniel's lessons" into the system. Whenever I found an empty field in my chart or a minus sign - which means I caught myself neglecting the lesson on a given day - I knew I needed to pay extra attention to his lessons, because it was me who slacked off this time.

I encourage you to imitate my system, because it is really simple and it takes virtually no time to use. Unless of course, you already have a tracking system of your own. If you use a different tool for similar purposes, like an application on your mobile to check off your to-do tasks, then just incorporate tracking the teaching sessions into it.

You may have other ideas on how to achieve a daily consistency more suitable for you and your child's temperament. For example, you could track together all the partial activities on the big board put on the wall in his/her room - reading, English, homework etc. Put happy or sad faces in the chart's cells. Make it fun and interesting for your kid to participate in tracking. Attach a system of rewards/penalties to it.

Do it your way. Use the method which is best suited for you to make a habit of the daily teaching session.

Just keep in mind the two bottom-line parameters of your tracking system - it must be fast and it must be easy to use.

You are a terribly busy parent, aren't you? So don't make the mistake of creating an overly complicated tracking tool. Let's say you picked an Evernote to track your daily "lessons," but you don't usually use it. Each time after your session with son/daughter, you turn on your old stationary computer, wait for the system to launch, put the password to log in, connect to the Internet, give your credentials to the Evernote app and fill the proper fields in it. Then you still have to turn off your computer. Did you get the image? Such an approach is totally missing the point of the tracking system!

If you miss the lesson, you must be able to catch yourself at it. That's why your tracking method must be habitual and easy to use.

6

---

# Conclusion

This booklet is not a textbook. I put my personal story in it, the insights into my family life, with one sole, single-minded purpose: to inspire you. If you see your child in trouble, if you feel helpless and don't know what to do, I've just given you a formula. Start. Persevere. Fine tune your methods. And do it until it works. Every sustained action brings results.

It's possible to change your child's future. It's doable, even if you have only 10 minutes a day. Even if you have neglected his/her education until now (that was what I did, I left Nathaniel's education in the hands of his teachers).

Kids need only a little encouragement, guidance, attention. Just be there.

Hey, if you are disappointed with my advice and my story, because you are doing much more for your kid, you are just a much better parent than me, take a look at it from another perspective: if such a poor excuse of a father as Michal could achieve so much, then what could **YOU** achieve?

If that thought inspires you to increase your efforts, I'm totally comfortable and happy with it.

I would appreciate you sending me an email with the news when you achieve something worth mentioning in your opinion - for example some progress of your child's education. I just want to know that my work helped one more person. A simple message to parent@onedollartips.com will be enough, although any other feedback is much welcomed, too. I'm also interested in some unique ways you've come up with to implement your individual educational program.

Take care. I don't wish you luck. I wish you to change your kid's destiny and personal satisfaction, and to know that it was you who helped in making it possible.

Don't miss the full story of Nathaniel's struggles in the next chapter.

# 7

# Nathaniel's Story

To put it simply, Nathaniel hasn't a scholar's inclinations. He is very active, he likes sports, he loves to play outside with other children. He has very little interest in books, he would much rather watch movies.

The first three grades of primary school weren't a problem for him. He is a bright guy. He could read even before he started school. He is a kind of math genius. As an 8-year-old, he could multiply two-digit numbers in memory.

We noticed his tendency to slack off, but he was always able to catch up. It was disturbing, but not alarming. He was generally a "B" level student. He was smarter than that and he often got "As", but he occasionally got "Cs" and even some "Ds", too.

But the brightness and talent could bring him only so far. The problems began for him in the 4th grade.

In Poland, the shift between 3rd and 4th grade is quite radical. The first three grades are a kind of school incubator. Children learn just a few subjects - math, Polish, English, basics of natural science, PE and art. 80% of classes are conducted by one teacher who is responsible for a particular class. If a child is on good terms with this teacher, his/her life is much easier. And my son has a lot of personal charm.

The 4th grade is a whole different story. Several new subjects are introduced. There is a different teacher for each subject. Pupils have to move around the school from one lesson to another. But those are just additional distractions. The main shift is that kids really need to start comprehending what they are taught.

And it is a lot of effort for a 10-year-old kid who didn't have to try to learn very hard in the past.

Nathaniel did what we do unconsciously when we are given the choice - he took the easy way. He didn't learn, he didn't read, he did his homework only when it was necessary - well, not even so often. He used every possible excuse facing his teachers.

In Poland, the primary school pupil is allowed to be unprepared for a lesson - may have no homework done, have no idea how to answer the question from the last lesson - twice per semester. It is a privilege reserved for extraordinary situations - the child was on a trip with family, sickness, something important had happened and the kid forgot or was unable to fulfill his obligations.

Nathaniel used almost all his "unpreparations" within the first seven weeks of the semester. He also got some negative grades because of lack of homework or lack of knowledge. But the worst of it was that he lied to us. When asked about homework, he had been saying - with a poker face - there was none or he did it flawlessly. He pretended that everything was all right. He made it to the last possible moment - when I was going to the first parent teacher meeting I told him it was his final chance to confess his actual school sins. "Everything is all right," he lied.

Half an hour later, I discovered that it wasn't.

We had a very turbulent evening that night. Nathaniel got grounded. I decided that we needed more control over his learning process. I started going through his backpack (and new lessons) almost every day. Whenever I found homework to do or already done, we either did it together or I marked it. As you know from previous chapters, I quickly identified his weak spots and started a few disciplines to neutralize them. Reading, memorizing English words, spelling, calligraphy and so on.

The first breakthrough came just two weeks later. I set him the goal of reading 100 words per minute by the end of the month. I didn't really believe he was capable of such progress (it's an over 40% increase) and neither did he. But - surprise, surprise - sustained action brings results. He was reading several pages a day for 13 days and it made all the difference.

It was a blessing. The first weeks were very tense. He was ashamed of himself, we were angry at him and the initial effort of implementing our teaching program was tiresome for both of us.

Nathaniel hated reading. I had to almost sit on him to make him read. Suddenly, he discovered he could improve by a simple daily practice. His attitude changed a bit. He was looking forward to the next reading exam, being confident that he was able to cope with it and to get the reward. I could ease up a little on reading and place my attention on other areas of his education.

Then another effect of our program became visible - his grades improved almost immediately. He is smart, he just needed to put some more effort into the learning process. He did it and he reaped the fruits of his labors.

I set him a 130 wpm reading goal for the end of November. He succeeded again, so he was allowed more time to play on the computer and most importantly, he was happy about himself, because he achieved something extraordinary: an 83% improvement in reading speed within six weeks. His confidence in himself grew.

Then came December, the month of winter holidays and Nathaniel was doing well, so I let go the pressure a little. My mistake.

I eased up on me. I had more time for different activities. And my son took advantage of it. In January, I was at another, not very optimistic, parent-teacher meeting. But his situation still was much better than in October. He was at risk of a "C" in only two subjects, and he generally achieved his solid "B" level as during the first three grades.

At the end of the first semester, he had to make up for some lessons and he only got a "C" in Natural

Science. That was far better than October's gloomy predictions.

We continued our program with its ups and downs. I tell you, his results were directly proportional to the effort I was willing to put into teaching. When I eased up just a little, so did he. When I put in more time and commitment, he did, too.

From January to April, he was in a "frustration period." First of all, he didn't understand why he had to learn and practice skills daily. He was satisfied with his previous level at school and was content, so what was the reason of further "torment?" Second, his progress in reading came to a standstill. He had read 120-130 words per minute since the beginning of December and he couldn't improve. This lack of result discouraged him a lot and the only power which kept him at reading practices was my determination. For several weeks, we established the ritual, the contest of will. When I got home from work, I would ask him, "Have you read today?"

"Not yet" - was his standard answer.

"Then do so." - and he did comply, grudgingly.

Needless to say, if I forgot to ask, he "forgot to read" that day.

To discourage him further, another disaster came. He was sick for a week and he forgot to ask a schoolmate about math homework. He didn't know about it, so he didn't do it. He got four or five "Fs because of it. And it was math, his favorite subject! The splendor of education was not something he could appreciate then.

During that period, we met with a pedagogue and psychologist a few times to determine if he was dyslexic. They said he was too young to determine that with certainty, but they saw he had some troubles with writing and spelling. They also estimated his IQ level as above average and ascertained he had extraordinary math skills. They advised to practice reading and spelling to improve his weak spots.

And we practiced.

Another breakthrough was involved with reading, too. In the middle of April, we were preparing for another reading test, when I proposed:

"Use your finger as a pointer." - this is another basic speed reading technique, but I had never mentioned it to him before. I had been focusing on eliminating his excessive sub-vocalization.

"OK" - he agreed hesitantly. He had never done it before.

And BAM! His result was 170 words per minute!

It gave both of us motivation to continue, to keep our efforts going. At the end of June, he achieved 192 words per minute, his life record up to now.

As usual, after the success came the failure. Nathaniel was so confident in his skill that he neglected his practice. And I was foolish enough to leave it in his hands. His results declined and we came back to the same old routine. I started to examine him from the text he had read on a daily basis, and I found it a good time to correct his speech mannerisms.

Another parent-teacher meeting wasn't very encouraging. Admittedly he had more "As" than "Bs", but he added some more "Cs" and "Ds" to the collection. The worst situation was in regard to Natural Science - "C" for the first semester and only one "C" and one "D" this semester. We had less than two months to fix it.

I snapped out of complacency and got to work. Still about 5-20 minutes a day. I just didn't have more time. But our activities were well rehearsed from times past. I just put more attention on our teaching program, and Nathaniel noticed that I was more serious and he got the message. Nothing fancy, nothing new, just consistency.

The only addition to our program was a short (just a few minutes long) Natural Science rehearsal session twice a week. He was supposed to learn it every day.

I don't have any idea how Nathaniel did it, but he set his marks right for the Natural Science class, as well as a bunch of other subjects. He finished the school year with honors! He got a "B" in Natural Science and English. The rest were "As"!

He also got the motivation to learn better in the next school year. My other son, Christopher, had a better average than him and he got a "scholarship," more of an award than a scholarship – thirty bucks given solemnly by the school director. However, the bucks had much more to do with this motivation than solemnity. ;)

That should constitute the happy end of his story, but life goes on ... I eased up on him again. It was the summer holiday after all! But the June's reading test revealed a drastic decrease in his reading speed, so for the past two months, I have made sure that he reads every day. He has read two more books, about 300 pages. I saw also to adding a new English word to his vocabulary every day.

The new school year is coming. I'm steeling myself to continue our teaching program. Nathaniel wants to get a scholarship - at least he says so. We will see.

## Update

I wrote the book during the summer holiday of 2013 and, since then, Nathaniel has slacked off once again.

October's parent-teacher meeting wasn't much better than the previous year. But still ... a little better.

He got grounded again. But he fixed his marks almost instantly this time. At the beginning of December, it seems that he is going to get only three "Bs" at the end of the semester. And knowing his magic ability to improve the grades at the last possible moment, maybe he will even exceed those expectations.

# Free Gift for You

Thanks for reading all the way to the end. If you made it this far, you must have liked it!

I really appreciate having people all over the world take interest in the thoughts, ideas, research, and words that I share in my books. I appreciate it so much that I invite you to visit: www.michalzone.com, where you can register to receive all of my future releases absolutely free.

You won't receive any annoying emails or product offers or anything distasteful by being subscribed to my mailing list. This is purely an invite to receive my future book releases for free as a way of saying thanks to you for taking a sincere interest in my work.

Once again, that's www.michalzone.com

# One Small Favor

I used to actively discourage my readers from giving me a review immediately after they read my book. I asked you for a review only once you began seeing results. This approach was against common sense and standard practice. Reviews are crucial for a book's visibility on Amazon. And my approach severely hindered me from getting my message out to people just like you, who stand to benefit from it.

I was convinced about that when "Master Your Time in 10 Minutes a Day" became a best-seller. Essentially, I've gotten a number of reviews in a short amount of time, but most of those reviews were the 'plastic' ones we all dislike on Amazon: "Great book! Great content! Great reading! Great entertainment!" Such reviews simply don't carry much weight; anybody could leave a review like that without even reading the book.

In the end, it didn't matter, and my book skyrocketed up the best-seller ranks, anyway. More people than ever have had the chance to get my book in their hands. I'm grateful for this, because more people have received the means to take control over their time and their destiny.

I want to ask a favor of you. If you have found value in this book, please take a moment and share your opinion with the world. Just let me know what you learned and how it affected you in a positive way. Your reviews help me to positively change the lives of others. Thank you!

# About the Author

I'm Michal Stawicki and I live in Poland, Europe. I've been married for over 14 years and am the father of two boys and one girl. I work full time in the IT industry, and recently, I've become an author. My passions are transparency, integrity and progress.

In August 2012, I read a book called "The Slight Edge" by Jeff Olson. It took me a whole month to start implementing ideas from this book. That led me to reading numerous other books on personal development, some effective, some not so much. I took a look at myself and decided this was one person who could surely use some development.

In November of 2012, I created my personal mission statement; I consider it the real starting point of my progress. Over several months time, I applied several self-help concepts and started building inspiring results: I lost some weight, greatly increased my savings, built new skills and got rid of bad habits while developing better ones.

I'm very pragmatic, a "down to earth" person. I favor utilitarian, bottom-line results over pure artistry. Despite the ridiculous language, however, I found there is value in the "hokey-pokey visualization" stuff and I now see it as my mission to share what I have learned.

My books are not abstract. I avoid going mystical as much as possible. I don't believe that pure theory is what we need in order to change our lives; the Internet age has proven this quite clearly. What you will find in my books are:

- detailed techniques and methods describing how you can improve your skills and drive results in specific areas of your life
- real life examples
- personal stories

So, whether you are completely new to personal development or have been crazy about the Law of Attraction for years, if you are looking for concrete strategies, you will find them in my books. My writing shows that I am a relatable, ordinary guy and not some ivory tower guru.

Made in the USA
Columbia, SC
20 June 2021